DAVID GOGGINS BOOK

The Biography of David Goggins

University Press

CONTENTS

INTRODUCTION

As a successful podcaster, Joe Rogan was used to odd encounters with his guests. Since 2015, The Joe Rogan Experience has been at the top of the podcast charts because of how entertaining and unpredictable it can be. Rogan had spent two decades as a standup comedian, so there was an expectation of humor with each of his podcasts, but there were plenty of times when his podcast would take a more serious turn. That was inevitable for a long-form conversation podcast that frequently included his friends and guests who brought a host of unknown experiences with them to the table.

His guest for that day was someone who had a complicated history and a reputation for his athletics. When Rogan entered the studio to prepare for the podcast, he quickly realized that he had no idea how unpredictable the talk would be. The former military man and current ultramarathon runner David Goggins was doing what he always did - he worked out his nervous energy. As Rogan walked into the studio, he froze when his eyes landed on Goggins. The podcast guest was really comfortable, as he had removed his shirt and was doing chin-ups to bide his time. Rogan would later comment, "You're the only guy I've ever had in the studio where when I showed up you were working out!"

Goggin's response was his typical simple answer, "That's who I am. That's my life." It was clear from that response that it was hardly the first time someone had been surprised by how dedicated Goggins was to fitness. Working out, running, and otherwise refining himself mentally and physically has been his life for several years now, and he is constantly working to keep himself healthy. As Rogan pointed out later in the 2018 interview, Goggins has hardened himself mentally to the point of being able to do things that everyone else would consider impossible.

The person he is today does not reflect who he was years ago, and he has no problem admitting that he was once a very different person. Growing up, no one would have predicted he would become an icon of fitness and impressive physical accomplishments. He once described his younger self, saying, "A lot of people put a title on me. They see me now as the guy with his shirt off who can do 4,030 pull-ups in 17 hours, who can run 205 miles in 39 hours, but what they don't understand is, one, I was just the opposite of who I am today...I was that guy who ran away from absolutely everything." Things clearly did not come so easily to him, and he suffered many failures and setbacks to reach where he is today.

From the young man who "ran away from absolutely everything," to the powerhouse of discipline and determination, David Goggins is a unique example of what a person can do if they focus. From his difficult childhood to earning a place in the military to personal loss, he lived a full and varied life by the time he reached his mid-40s. His story is inspirational, partly because of how many challenges he has overcome since childhood.

Having grown up in a troubled family, he worked hard to start a military career, first as a part of the Air Force, then as a Navy Seal and Army Ranger. He served during a time of war and experienced personal loss that still affects him. After leaving the military, he transitioned from soldier to runner and endurance athlete. Today, he has authored a book about his experiences to help others. He has appeared as a guest across different media platforms to discuss what matters most to him. Part of his work is earning money for a charity to help the children of fallen military service members. He continues to inspire people while benefiting the causes that matter to him most. And along with everything else, he continues to participate in athletic events.

CHAPTER 1

Early Life

On February 17, 1975, Jacking Goggins gave birth to her second son, David Goggins, at Millard Fillmore Hospital. At the time, the family had four members, though only three of the four were close or on good terms. The father of the family, Trunnis Goggins, was reportedly an aggressive man who seemed to take a much more old-world view of the way family should be, and his expectations for his family focused on him. David had an older brother, Trunnis Jr. The four lived outside of Buffalo, New York, in a small town called Williamsville. Even in the 1970s, Buffalo, NY, had a thriving black community, but moving out to the city's suburbs saw increasingly smaller diverse populations. Like many suburbs at the time, many white families had moved out of cities and into the surrounding areas. To show just how much diversity the suburbs lacked, Goggins was the first

African American baby born in his hospital, which wasn't far from his parent's home - a middle-class community called East Amherst.

He and his mother would be discharged from the hospital, and not much is covered over the next few years. Jackie, Trunnis Jr., and David would live with their father in the small suburb for a few years, and David would later describe this period as nightmarish. It's possible that he faced some problems because of his race, but he has not indicated that he had any particular trouble with people outside of the home – it was the threat from within. What should have been a safe place would instead create terrible memories for his mother, brother, and himself.

The way his father treated them resulted in David becoming a quiet child, once describing himself as "very scared, insecure, stuttering, and getting beat up by his dad." From nearly the beginning of his life, David seemed to learn to fear his father, which could have translated into how he interacted with the rest of the world. With his home not feeling safe, he did not notice problems outside of his home. It is likely that even if things weren't as easy for him around the community, it was far safer than what he experienced at home.

For a large part of his early life, his father was an ever-present and threatening figure who would affect him over the course of his life. Initially, this was a negative effect, but as he aged and learned how to deal with the trauma from his youth, the inspiration would help form the man known for doing physically impossible feats.

A Father's Iron Fist

Looking at his house from the outside, it would be impossible to guess what went on behind the façade. It had the kind of suburban aesthetic that suggested that the family within lived the American dream. The neighborhood was full of expansive, luscious green homes with trees and double garages to suggest that it was a place for families who were stable and successful. Walking down the street would make the pedestrian feel safe and secure as families played in their yards, children biked up and down the street, and a sense of peace surrounded them. It was more like a safe harbor to relax after spending time in the bustling city of Buffalo.

The serenity of the neighborhood was erased once a family member stepped inside, where their father ruled with an iron fist. As Goggins would later say, his father was both a tyrant and a criminal, which wasn't an exaggeration as that was the profession his father had chosen. When describing what it was like living with his father, Goggins compared his father to Denzel Washington's character Frank Lucas in *American Gangster*. While Washington has typically played heroes, he has a few villain characters that have left the audience uncomfortable with their antics. In Training Day, Alonzo Harris's villainous character is probably his best-known bad guy character, and he is a corrupt cop who abuses his power to gain money. By comparison, the character Frank Lucas didn't even have the cover of a respectable job. He was a drug smuggler who built an entire empire following the end of the Vietnam War in the late 60s and early 70s. Lucas's criminal career made him millions of dollars and gave him a name that was feared and respected, but it also left behind numerous murder victims and assassinations. The comparison was not meant to suggest that his father was murderous, but Goggins saw a lot of similarities between the villainous character and his own father. In fact, most of the other aspects of the character were accurate in terms of how Goggins saw his father. "He was that bad," Goggins said in one of the interviews where he made the comparison.

What probably connected the two for Goggins was that his father was a criminal, and he ran prostitutes from the nearby Canadian border into Buffalo. It's not quite the same as drugs, but it has some significant ethical implications and is incredibly illegal. David described his dad as a "big-time pimp, big-time hustler, big-time anything bad." How much of his father's work Goggins understood when he was young is unclear, but the element of the criminal world that made it inside the home was the violence that most people associate with the criminal world.

Goggins has many memories of his father beating him and his brother. His father would also assault their mother, which Goggins found especially difficult to witness. "One time, my mom got knocked out on top of stairs," Goggins once said. "And he dragged her down the stairs by her hair. I was six years old. I'll never forget that." Another memory he had was when he decided to stick up for his mother. As he watched his father physically abuse his mother, Goggins decided he couldn't just stand by and watch. He hurried down the stairs where his father was abusing Jackie. Once he was close enough, Goggins jumped on his father's back. Immediately, his father's violence shifted to his child. As Jackie watched her husband beat her son, she realized their life could not continue as it had been because she didn't know when her husband would kill one of them.

Wanting Something More

Before the family's dynamic reached a breaking point, Goggins was already aware that his life was untenable. The kids were hurt by more than just the occasional acts of violence. In addition to his criminal activities, his father also owned a skating rink with a bar on the second floor. Of course, he didn't feel he needed to hire many staff members because he had three people whom he could force to work for free whenever he needed them. David and his brother would work with the patrons who came to the skating rink from when it opened until it closed around 10:00 pm. Once the rink closed, their work shifted from customer service to being janitors around the rink. They were expected to clean the entire place, including scraping gum off the floors, managing the garbage, cleaning up some of the bathrooms, and making sure the place was presentable for the next day. As the two boys finished cleaning up the rink, their parents headed upstairs to manage the bar. After working well after most children's bedtime, the two brothers would find a place downstairs to sleep until their parents were finished upstairs. The bar closed at 3:00 am. Then their parents would have to finish cleaning up before they were ready to go home. That meant that the children had a very interrupted sleep schedule.

All this child labor had a detrimental effect on their schooling. They rarely went to school. On those occasions where they did make it to school, it was obvious that they had not regularly attended, to the point where it became virtually impossible for them to catch up to their peers. On top of that, David believed he had a learning disability that kept him from fully understanding the topics they did learn in class. "When I went to school," he admitted during one interview, "I had to deal with my learning disability, and I had social anxiety. I was just a jacked-up kid from living in this tortured home."

Most people outside David's family didn't know what he was enduring in his home life. They lived in the suburbs in a safe place, but the skating rink and bar were in one of the seedier parts of Buffalo. This provided two very different worlds, so there wasn't a single community where the family lived. This meant they divided their days so no one could get to know them or see the problems. "We worked around mostly blacks and I lived around mostly whites, but no one knew what was going on in the house that was on 201 Paradise Road."

Despite living with the fear and chaos that came with working much of his days, David always felt he was meant for something more, even though he didn't know what that might be. He described it as a voice in the back of his mind, telling him he needed to get up and move to work to find something else. He needed to keep pushing forward to accomplish something. It would be a few years before he'd start taking that voice seriously, but it was there from an early age, pushing him to keep going and endure what must have felt like an endless cycle that would make anyone feel hopeless.

That change would finally come when his mother decided it was simply too risky for her children to stay around such an abusive man. Abused women are usually pushed to finally leave their abusive husbands because they fear their husbands will kill their children. It is often the final straw. They can take the risk with their own lives but are unwilling to put their children's lives on the line. After seeing her husband abusing her son in a way that made her worried that Goggins would end up getting killed, Jackie began to take steps to get her and her children out of the danger they faced at home. She was likely dreaming of a house where they would finally have a safe haven. With that in mind, Goggins's mother began planning their escape.

CHAPTER 2

Escape

Brazil, Indiana, is a small town that most people have never heard about. In the 2010 census, the town had a population of just under 8,009, a culture shock coming from the small city of Buffalo, NY, with a population of over 260,000.

Yet this is exactly Goggins's experience as his mother decided to escape from the abusive home. Taking both of her sons, she left for this small place where it would be much harder for her husband to find them. Initially, this seemed to remove the root of all of their family problems. It meant that the family had a chance at happiness.

Unfortunately, it wasn't quite the escape that his mother had hoped to pull off. They had left the tyrant and criminal behind, but all small towns come with their own problems. Brazil was no different, creating a whole new world of problems for a family trying to get back on their feet. As a result, his life did not suddenly change for the better. Instead, Goggins would later describe the change, saying, "That's when the real war started for me."

It is important to note that Goggins only speaks of problems when he discusses his time in Brazil. There were good points about the small town that provided stability for the family. When discussing what it was like, he is always quick to point out that "Brazil is a small town with great people—a lot of great people. But there were about 10 black families out of about 10,000 people in the town." As one could imagine, that meant the African American families would often feel like outsiders. This might seem like something that wouldn't be a problem considering they had been a significant minority in the suburbs of Buffalo. The primary difference was that they could go into Buffalo and find many people with similar experiences and cultures. Unfortunately, there was no similar community close to their new home.

The real problem with their new town was there were more hostile attitudes toward African Americans in Indiana than they had experienced in New York. The racism they faced was much more obvious to Goggins at that time. It seemed that there was more racism in their suburban town than he remembered, but living with his abusive father made it far less memorable. The trauma of living with an abuser eliminates the safe haven most people have, making it less likely that people will notice problems outside the home that aren't so obviously dangerous. Now they lived in a town with a much safer home environment, making it far easier to notice when there are other problems. Brazil did seem safe enough to more openly display their racism because there were far fewer African American and minority families within the space where it was easy to travel. There wasn't the kind of robust African American community that could provide a sense of security. Any racism that Goggins may have experienced in the suburbs would likely have been subtle, and while insidious on some levels, it didn't create the kinds of undertones of danger that would be made much more obvious in Brazil. The most obvious example of the kinds of more obvious racism practiced in Brazil is the KKK march that occurred during the 4th of July parade in 1995. This would be a more open and shocking example of the majority race ensuring they cowed over all other races who lived in the area. The family now had a sense of safety when they were together, but there would have been a sense of fear at all times because they knew that the racist terrorist group was active in their area. Although the KKK may not have been as openly violent in the 1980s and 1990s as before the *Civil Rights Movement*, they were still violent towards other races, particularly African Americans. They were just more careful so that they could get away with their horrific acts.

Goggins clearly states that he isn't referring to the entire town when discussing how ostracized he felt. Not everyone in the town was openly and obviously racist, and he encountered many people who treated him mostly like anyone else. Many great people were friendly with him and his family, so it wasn't like they felt fear toward everyone they encountered: "Some of the best people I knew were there. But there's also a lot of racism there, too. It kind of haunts you." This would likely have been a bit more difficult on some level because it would be nearly impossible to know who to trust. Encountering people outside of the home made a child question their safety because racism was far less acceptable. Those who held those beliefs would likely keep them hidden until they were in a situation where they felt they could be more open about their beliefs. When in a group, that would increase the likelihood of them turning violent against someone of a different race. This would create a different sense of fear and uncertainty in a child, especially since they would have to learn that there was a problem with their new home that they had not encountered in their previous town.

There were significant trades in their situation and condition in Brazil. The children were free to attend school regularly in the small town because they were no longer forced to work late into the night cleaning a skating rink. It was certainly a very different experience to have the ability to go to school, but it came with a completely new set of concerns. Schools were no longer a place where they felt incapable because of their home life but a place to be afraid for their safety. The type of racism that some of the students learned at home came into the school with them, and they did not have a problem inflicting their racist beliefs onto the few minority children who attended their primarily white schools. The racist expressions began to inflict upon the two boys nearly from the beginning of their time in the town. Goggins remembers turning away from his work to talk to someone and then turning back to see that someone had anonymously written racial threats on his notebooks and desk. This covert and blatant racism would be incredibly concerning because getting away with something once encourages people to escalate their horrible behavior. Dealing with this kind of regular harassment would be terrifying for anyone, particularly for children who had just escaped a life-threatening situation. Though he had not attended school often in New York, he had not experienced anything like this. The shock and fear it instilled have stuck with him over the years, which is why he is so open about the racism he faced. Goggins also feels it is important to note that it isn't everyone, which is a differentiated take on the situation. Perhaps he can take this approach because he doesn't want to perpetuate the wrong-headed assumptions leading to the racist bullying he faced.

Recognizing it wasn't everyone helps keep people from immediately getting on the defensive. It also shows that he does have some positive sentiments about the town, even if his memories are largely marred by the racism he experienced nearly from the time they arrived.

As should be expected, when people have continued to get away with bad behavior for years, the racist students would escalate their actions against him. When he reached high school, Goggins did manage to have a car that he was allowed to drive to school. One day, he returned to his car to find that the racists had scrawled a death threat all over his car. It is the kind of thing that makes a person paranoid and can affect them for the rest of their life. Goggins is very open about how it affected him, saying, "All the insecurities I had when I was a kid with my father just got worse in this new area. It got worse and worse and worse, and it haunted me."

In addition to the racism and threats of violence, his family experienced poverty. Compared to where they lived before, their situation was completely different, though it was possibly worth it on some levels. Unfortunately, the now single-parent household had to trade financial stability for physical security, something that no family should have to do to feel safe in their own homes. When thinking back, Goggins would say, "For a while, we lived in the government subsidized apartments, seven dollars a month," indicating just how different their new places as compared to their previous house where there were greater levels of privacy (though that privacy also meant their father was able to do more without being heard). In addition to the subsidized housing, they were on food stamps. In an effort to make up for the significant financial changes, their mother worked hard to provide a happier life. Her hard work eventually saw their fortunes turn, and the three-person family moved into an apartment that charged $230 a month.

What became far more clear during this time was Goggin's learning disability. Since he had not spent nearly so much time in school in New York, it was likely easy to think that he was learning slowly because of his large number of absences and lack of consistency in his education. When he was young, learning disabilities were not nearly as well recognized as they are today. Even if there had been more support, his family would not have had the money to get him the help he needed. Once he realized he was still having trouble, Goggins turned to the one thing that would ensure that he didn't really learn – he began cheating. As an adult, he has looked back and is ashamed that he relied on cheating throughout his school years. "It's kind of humbling to talk with my stories sometimes," he told one interviewer as he admitted to regularly cheating. "It's embarrassing, but it's real. It's who I am, and it's what I am." His typical method of cheating was not limited to just tests but to "every assignment and every test" from fourth grade all the way through high school to pass classes and keep moving forward.

Despite the negative aspects of his life following the move to Brazil, he continued to hear that voice pushing him to do more and be better. "It kept talking louder and louder and louder," he says, "But I was doing nothing about it." Finally, that desire to do more with his life brought him to a tipping point that finally saw him acting. As he puts it, "I decided to make moves." The problem was he had to determine what that path forward would be.

CHAPTER 3

Air Force

Initially, that path was one that many people in similar situations have taken - David chose to enter the military. It was a life that could give him the structure, discipline, and stability he desperately lacked in his childhood and teenage years. He did stray from the typical choice, though. Where many go into the Marines or the Army, Goggins decided on the Air Force, and with that decision was a host of other challenges as he struggled to achieve his first goal as an adult.

He began down the path as soon as he finished high school, and he knew exactly what he wanted to do if he was successful in his attempt to join this particular military branch. As he would explain in one interview, "I wanted to be an Air Force pararescueman. The guys that jump out of airplanes and save downed pilots. It's a special operator in the Air Force." This job would help him stand out because it requires that participants meet a very high bar to join. In addition to recovering downed pilots, this is an elite group who work with NASA and are most typically the personnel called to recover astronauts after water landings. Pararescue men are often called PJs, short for "para jumpers."

To become a PJ, participants are expected to be in peak physical fitness and must meet very high standards in various fields. They are also expected to have Navy Seal levels of water skills because they are expected to go on significant dives in difficult conditions. Before becoming eligible to take the courses to become a PF, Goggins first must pass a test to join the Air Force.

Passing The Test

Anyone wishing to join the Air Force must pass the Armed Services Vocational Aptitude Battery, better known as the ASVAB. David described it as a "watered-down SAT." Though this makes it sound like an easy test, the ASVAB isn't particularly easy for a large percentage of people, and it was particularly difficult for someone with a learning disability. Like the SAT, the test isn't going to be easy for everyone, but unlike the SAT, it was entirely possible to fail this test. Goggins' learning disability was further compounded by the fact that he hadn't learned how to learn because he had successfully relied on his ability to cheat for years. For the ASVAB, Goggins couldn't just copy the answers from somewhere else because everyone is given a different test to prevent cheating. It didn't take him long to realize this, so he had to go into the test and take it without any real preparation. Like many people who try to take the SAT without any preparation or with an expectation that they could cheat, his first test results ensured that he wouldn't be getting into the Air Force for the foreseeable future. "I got like 20," he told one interviewer. While this is a horrible grade, it did at least give him a starting point. Since he would have to learn how to learn, it would be easier going forward to see how successful he was in this particular endeavor. More importantly, he didn't give up after this abysmal result. It doesn't seem like he realized that he needed to take the time to learn yet, though, as he took the ASVAB a second time soon after the first, scoring an 18.

With such an underwhelming result the second time, Goggins knew that his new path was already at great risk of being a failure. People are only allowed to take the ASVAB three times; after that, they are not allowed to take it again. Realizing that he couldn't just bluff his way through and knowing that cheating wasn't an option, the only solution available to him was to get help.

The ASVAB is a multiple-choice exam. The scoring isn't based on the number of answers you get right but on how you performed compared to everyone else. The Air Force only accepts above-average recruits for those who took the test. A contributing factor to the test being difficult is that it is offered to high schoolers, and they are given time out of their regular schedule to take it. That meant some teenagers took the test without any interest in joining, only to get out of class. This means competing against a bigger pool of people, some of whom have no desire to do anything with their score. For Goggins, someone who had always been behind the curve in school, this would be a major challenge to outperform a majority of test takers. Fortunately, he had someone in his corner willing to assist him as much as she could – his mother.

Despite their economic troubles, his mother hired a tutor to help him understand the questions and how to reach the desired answers. His tutor worked with him for an hour a week, and he had six months before taking the exam again. Unwilling to rely on his tutor to help him pass, Goggins dedicated much time to studying.

It was grueling in a way that he had never experienced. To this point, most of his struggles had been more survival based. Now he was fighting to follow a path that he knew would put him in mortal danger if he succeeded – and he was inspired to work hard. This time he was working hard for himself instead of an abusive father.

All of his work paid off when he finally passed the test. However, that was just the first hurdle out of the way.

Training Begins

Within the Air Force, the training process to become a PJ is informally known as "Superman School" because it is so difficult. The name seems apt because the vast majority of soldiers that enter the program, which takes place at the Pararescue Indoctrination Training Center, drop out long before the training is finished. The difficulty of the training would become very clear within those first two months. One hundred fifty people entered the program when Goggins joined. Within the first six weeks, there were only about 50 left.

Upon first looking into the training, jumping out of an airplane would rank high on the list of difficult aspects of the training. However, that was one of the easiest parts. The real challenges were physically punishing. Trainees go through what is called "water confidence training," a grueling experience where each trainee is taken almost to the point of drowning. For example, they have to swim for hours at a time. They wear diving goggles filled with water, so they get the sensation of being underwater even when their heads are above the surface. They must recover goggles and a snorkel tube from the bottom of a deep pool and "clear" them by filling them with air while still underwater. These are just a few of the tasks that must be completed, and they are far from the hardest things that trainees are expected to complete.

Like many other trainees, this was the hardest part of the training for Goggins. "I was terrified of the water," he says. Even though he'd learned to swim, the water confidence training felt like drowning all the time, keeping him in a near-perpetual state of terror. "All of our lives we've been breathing, and they take that from you," David would explain in an interview years later. "They want to see how comfortable you are in the water."

Part of why this was so difficult for Goggins was because of his race. It's a cultural phenomenon that's been studied repeatedly in recent years, but many members of his race in both the US and the UK are either unable to swim or very poor at it. While there is some evidence that some races have negative buoyancy due to a difference in bone density, many now feel this is more culturally motivated than anything else. It does play into a stereotype, but there is a significant difference between learning to swim and being comfortable in the water. A large factor why swimming is less common for African Americans is because there were long stretches in US history where they were prohibited from entering swimming pools. If African American parents never learned to swim, they couldn't pass down that necessary knowledge and comfort level in the water to their children. It's a case of a stereotype that proves itself right even though it really shouldn't.

Being in the water and fearing to drown is far more prevalent for people who don't grow up exposed to swimming environments. A large part of the problem for him was that he and many people in his community didn't spend much time in the water. That would be a significant contributing factor to feeling more afraid of drowning. This could be beneficial, though, as people who are incredibly confident in their swimming abilities are more likely to drown because of overconfidence in their abilities. A more cautious and calculated approach improves the odds of surviving in the water.

No matter the reason, David struggled greatly with the swimming portion of the training. "I wanted to quit so badly," he admitted, "But I'd quit everything in my life, I'd copied through school, I'd always run away. Now, I want to prove people wrong."

Goggins has said that over those six weeks, he barely slept. Though that time, the little voice in his head pushed him to keep going through the fear and sleep deprivation. Unfortunately, this time pushing through the situation wasn't enough to find the success he desperately wanted.

CHAPTER 4

Setback

T hough his mind and spirit were willing, Goggins' body could not achieve what he wanted. While his race shouldn't have played any meaningful role in his ability to swim – African Americans can learn to swim just as adeptly as other races when given the same amount of access and comfort in water – there was one decisive downside to a well-known genetic disease that is almost exclusive to people who have African heritage. The vast majority of people with sickle cell traits and sickle cell anemia have African ancestors, which is a problem when it comes to more extreme types of swimming.

Complete Breakdown

As training continued, Goggins seemed to have just

as much trouble with the water training as when he had started. Realizing that something more problematic could occur, one of the military doctors ran tests on Goggins to determine if something physical prevented the trainee from experiencing the excepted improvements in his abilities. When it was found out that Goggins had a sickle cell trait, the military knew that more needed to be done before the trainee could continue. This is different from sickle-cell anemia, which can kill someone. The trait can occur in only one of the two alleles (part of a gene) needed for the full disease. Even so, having the trait can be dangerous and more tests would be needed to determine if David was fit to continue his training.

As a result of these findings, David was pulled out of training for a full week. He stated that the week out of training was very strange. On the one hand, he felt a sense of relief not to be in the water, but on the other hand, he had to sit on the sidelines and watch his fellow trainees every day as they progressed and often improved.

Having put so much effort into finding a way to be comfortable in the water, it felt like a low blow. Just when he felt like he was getting there, he was now benched for a week, starting that cycle of stress again. During that time, he struggled with a desire to just quit. After all, he wasn't sure if he could muster up the courage to get in that water again. But, given a full week to consider whether he wanted to continue, Goggins decided to continue the training. There were only three weeks left, and he was determined to conquer the problems he had with water.

What he didn't calculate into his decision was what it meant to lose a full week of training. He wouldn't be allowed to rejoin the group, completing the training with a week less than them. Nor would he be given his own training program that would pick up from where he had left off.

Goggins would have to start over from the beginning if he wanted to continue. That meant he would start from week one with an entirely new group of trainees, ending the training with more weeks than anyone else and repeating several weeks that had already been torturous.

That was too much for him. "I broke," David admitted, "I couldn't imagine going back through that again." Realizing that he couldn't start over again, he finally realized that he would have to take a different path, "I made up a lie. I told them that the sickle-cell thing was really scaring me." That was a lie because he was really afraid of the water training and not the sickle cell trait.

His superiors accepted the excuse and gave him a medical discharge from the training. But, despite the discharge, what happened was really not different from anyone else who had left – he had flunked out of the training.

Working With Tacp

With his initial desire to join the Pararescue training over, Goggins had to decide what he wanted to do. It wasn't a complete loss, though, as he was still part of the Air Force and had many other potential professional paths to take. He soon found a new job that fit him much better: working as a TACP Officer, which he did from age 19 to 22.

A TACP Officer, or a United States Air Force Tactical Air Control Party Officer, is an instrumental support member of the Air Force. They often work alongside Special Operation Forces and coordinate gunfire from naval ships and air support within mixed combat situations. Usually, a TACP Officer, or a group of them, is assigned to a unit from the US Army. They may coordinate and instruct airstrikes and air support for soldiers on the ground, acting as liaisons between the Army and the Air Force. And this was a great choice for him because he didn't spend all his time feeling like his life was at risk. When talking about what he ended up doing, Goggins reflected on it very favorably, "It was a cool job, but there's no water. I was afraid of the water, so I avoided it."

While David did like this work and stayed with it for several years, the fact that it was within his comfort zone ultimately led to the first major setback in his adulthood. "I gained 125 pounds during that time," David has said with obvious distress about that result. His weight reached almost 300 pounds, and he felt like it was because he had stayed within his comfort zone, which had a significant, negative effect on him physically. Finding that comfort zone was damaging to him mentally and emotionally, though it took longer to realize that. "I found things that were comfortable," he explains, "and the more comfortable things I found comfortable, the more uncomfortable my mind was."

Ultimately, he had expressed that a large part of his failings was because he had ignored the voice pushing him to do and be more; "There I was trying to avoid that conscience. I wanted to be left alone." Because of that pained conscience, David eventually chose to leave the Air Force because he wasn't accomplishing what he felt he could. Moreover, after all that initial work, he had become comfortably unhappy with his life.

CHAPTER 5

Floundering in Comfort

After leaving the Air Force, Goggins felt like his life was getting worse, even though, by all outside accounts, he was successful. He seemed to have risen above the difficulties of his past, but he still needed to manage to accomplish the things he felt he should have.

With no obvious direction, it became essential to establish a new goal and follow that to completion. This time, there would be no excuses or justifications for not following through with that goal. But, like his initial goal, this one would require a drastic and difficult transformation, one that was much harder than what he had done as a teenager. And one that meant changing his physical appearance and altering his mindset and identity.

At 24 years old, Goggins felt like he'd already given up on life, with all those early sacrifices being for nothing. Instead, he worked for a pest control company called Ecolabs, doing something that wasn't fulfilling and didn't push him to improve himself. The work was through the night, spraying for cockroaches at various restaurants and fast food places. It was a different kind of work than he had set out to do when he had managed to make it into the Air Force.

On his average day, he'd work through the night, spraying for cockroaches and looking for signs of rodents. Then, at 7 am, he'd head home. He managed to arrange his schedule so that he'd finish in the Stake' n Shake, so he could pick up a 42-ounce chocolate shake on the way home, demonstrating that he had not yet moved to get out of that comfort zone that had led to him leaving the military. Then he'd walk across the street to the Seven Eleven and buy a box of mini doughnuts. Finally, after an unhealthy series of food purchases, it was time to go home to eat all that junk food and watch TV before going to bed.

David described himself as "this big old fat guy," even though he was only 24 at the time. "Yeah, I worked out, but I was fat. I didn't run, didn't PT [work with a personal trainer], I just hit the gym."

Then, after he left work one morning and arrived home with his large shake and junk food, Goggins saw a show on Discovery Channel called Navy SEALS: BUDS Class 234: "That's when everything changed for me. I was taking a shower, and I walked out and heard these guys, and I watched the show, and it made me reflect big-time on who I was." That one show made it nearly impossible for him to ignore that voice demanding more of him.

Navy SEALS: BUDS Class 234 aired as a six-hour mini-series on Discovery Channel in 2000. It follows a group of Navy SEALs trainees through BUDS, one of Earth's most difficult training programs. BUDS is often referred to as Hell Week, and it is even more difficult than pararescue training. The vast majority of trainees give up before getting halfway through the training. If they feel they can't go on at any point in the process, they only have to ring a bell on the beach and are removed from the training program.

Goggins could not stop watching, "I saw these guys going into water, so the show made me feel terrified." Ever since that initial water confidence training, Goggins had avoided water. He hated going to the pool and swimming at the beach. But the water wasn't the only thing he avoided. Goggins has said that he had multiple fears—things he had to avoid in life, "And that's what created the person I am today." It became clear that he had spent his life running away from things. Having left the Air Force to improve himself, he hid behind a different kind of comfort while working with pest control. "I was watching these guys going through Hell Week, class 234, and these guys ringing the bell, quitting, dropping their helmet down, rolling out..." Seeing those who failed and gave up reminded Goggins of the person he'd been his whole life.

The Discovery Channel series showed not only those who walked away but those who stuck with it and kept going no matter what. "I saw real men," David said of the impression he got from watching, "Real men who were staying, who were overcoming adversity, who were overcoming all these different things." With this impression firmly implanted in his mind, Goggins realized he could step up and do better. "I had blamed so many people in my life for my fears: my dad, my mom, the people of Brazil, my learning disability, my own skin color... everything." But watching that show made him realize that "No one's gonna come to help me. This is me against me, period. I had to man up."

The emotions he felt watching the show flipped a switch, and he was finally ready to try again. Goggins desired to be more, to do more with his life. And this time, he set his sights even higher – he wanted to be a Navy SEAL.

CHAPTER 6

Tipping Point

From the show's inspiration, Goggins started facing all of his fears, one at a time. There was so much from his past that kept him up at night. Finally, he realized just how much he lived in a world of fear. That comfort zone he'd learned to stay in was just a place of protection from all of his fears and one that prevented him from actually moving forward with his life. It was like he was trapped in a bubble of fear, too afraid to move because he knew there was a lot of pain in the world. However, he was starting to realize that he could choose to face those fears instead of letting them define him.

The way he saw it, he had two choices to make. His first option was to continue as that 300-pound, 24-year-old guy who sprayed cockroaches and made a thousand dollars a month, staying in that comfort zone that would see him age and never improve. He knew that this option would mean that someday when he turned 50, he would look back on his life and realize he never became what he could have been.

He would say his second option was to "...totally just sack it up and fail and fail and fail until I succeed." This option would lead to him looking back over his life with a sense of satisfaction and accomplishment. It was the one he would ultimately choose.

He started facing fears at every opportunity. If something made him uncomfortable, he'd embrace it. If something were hard but would help him to grow, he would work through it until he was successful. Perhaps most importantly, he started calling recruiters, letting them know his goal was to become a Navy SEAL.

Every conversation with a recruiter went about the same, though, as each branch and section of the military has its own height and weight requirements. At 6 foot 1 and 297 pounds, Goggins was well outside of those requirements. Even though he'd served in the Air Force, which considered a positive reason to recruit him, once a recruiter learned about his weight, Goggins was no longer considered a possible recruit for active duty. Instead, some would say he should try to get into the reserves.

After several rejections, one recruiter decided to

consider Goggins if he could lose 106 pounds in less than three months. This would get the inspiring Navy SEAL into the next class and go through Hell Week.

It was the first significant trial of his goal and initially proved to be too much of a stumbling block. It is another instance of one of his interviews where he expresses disappointment in himself: "I gave up." After that talk, he decided to go back to spraying for cockroaches, figuring that losing so much weight in such little time would be impossible.

That sense of despair and fear of failure didn't stop him. As he got to work the next night, Goggins "hit the motherload of cockroaches," which made him stop and reflect on his life again. As he watched so many roaches scurry around in front of him, and knowing why he was there, he had a life-altering breakthrough - "this is my life." At that moment, he felt a strange sense of understanding and empathy with the creatures he was there to kill because, at that moment, he felt like an insect. They were scurrying to hide in a way that he understood because he felt that he was scurrying away from his fear. It had a deep impact on him.

As soon as he had this revelation, Goggins left the job. This meant leaving the spray canister on at the job so that he could go home and begin the process of getting rid of 106 pounds.

It was the last time he had a serious moment of

doubt; as he would describe later, "I became the most obsessed person on the planet earth."

CHAPTER 7

Becoming Goggins

The first day Goggins went for a run, he figured he'd be able to do about 4 miles. Even though he was almost 300 pounds, he had run and endured much worse. Getting through 4 miles seemed easy enough as he started to run, but he barely made it a quarter of a mile before he had to return home in a lot of pain.

It was an eye-opening experience, and he learned not to overestimate his abilities without considering his current physical condition. He was armed with the knowledge that he would need to be more reasonable in his approach to losing weight. He started running almost every day, adapting a more reasonable distance for someone who had to start from the beginning. To ensure he got enough exercise, Goggins spent about an hour on a bike while trying to reach a point where he could run longer distances. Knowing that weightlifting was a quick way of burning calories, he worked out at the gym, doing extremely high reps of relatively low weight. This demonstrated that he had learned that initial lesson well – he was taking care of his body so that he wasn't hurting it to the point where he would have to stop.

Little by little, the pounds started to burn off. As the weight came off, he realized that more than just losing weight was required to succeed because his body wasn't always the problem. To be successful in doing what he considered impossible, he had to change his mentality. Goggins felt he had to "become a guy that didn't exist, a guy that could take all the pain and suffering and judgment and use it to be better, like fuel." The way he did that was something that he recommends to people today, "I built this callous mind, and I built it through suffering."

As he pushed himself physically, Goggins would push his mind to do things outside his comfort zone. For example, he started running a 3:00 am no matter the conditions outside, even in the rain and the snow. He embraced all of the things that made him physically uncomfortable, which is incredibly difficult to do. If he didn't want to do something, he would push himself to do it, knowing that it was probably good for him and would help him grow as a person. While he was doing it to get into the Navy SEALs, it was a mentality that he could apply to nearly everything.

He lost the weight and returned to the recruiter to show that he had managed to get through the first major hurdle. From there, he got into the SEALS class and was cleared for Hell Week. With his new mentality and approach to life, Goggins went through three Hell Weeks in a single year. Unfortunately, he had to drop out the first time after contracting pneumonia, and the second time he had to drop out because of a stress fracture. This proved that he had come a long way since his time in the Air Force – he was willing to start over twice. And it was the last time he could try since trainees only got three chances. And this time, he was successful.

This was the journey that would come to define him and the way he would approach life: "I started realizing that my potential is almost endless. The mind is what you make it." The mental transformation he had to undergo to make substantial physical changes changed his perspective on who he was. Seeing himself in a new light, he changed his name uniquely and subtly: "Now, I was just Goggins." He has said that the name transformation was akin to Bruce Wayne becoming Batman, and it meant taking an approach to life that required him to act.

It helped Goggins as his second military career would lead to great tragedy and physical pain. But, with his new identity intact, Goggins had the mental strength to face any challenge.

CHAPTER 8

Running

O nce he became a SEAL, Goggins became the first to become a SEAL, completed US Army Ranger training, and was in the Air Force Tactical Air Controller Training. This distinction earned him recognition, and he seemed to be on track for a fantastic military career.

However, he was a member of the military, and he and his friends were deployed. This meant that they would be in danger, and in 2005 he lost several of his friends when their helicopter crashed. It was devastating, and Goggins decided that he needed to do something that would honor them. He decided that the best way to do that was to participate in the Badwater Ultramarathon after raising money for the Special Operations Warrior Foundation.

He was initially rejected because he didn't meet their requirements to join – what he did in the military did not count because it did not follow the same guidelines. This was a reason that he could work with, and Goggins began looking for something he could join to meet the requirement. He found an ultramarathon that was being held in San Diego and had a 24-hour time lime. Entering it, he joined and managed to run 101 miles in less than 19 hours. This was not enough to qualify for Badwater, though, so joined another marathon in Las Vegas. His time from this marathon finally gave him the qualifying times to enter. Now all he had to do was wait for the invitation. While he waited, he continued to raise money for his chosen cause. As he waited, he went to Hawaii to compete in another ultramarathon. He would finally get his invitation in 2006 after coming in second during the Ultraman World Championships Triathlon.

With his invitation, Goggins was ready to participate in a 135-mile course that would take him through Death Valley. One of the reasons his qualifications were so high was that between 20 and 40% of those invited failed to finish. For his first time in the competition, Goggins placed 5th, a feat no one else had managed in their first attempt.

Running wasn't the only way he challenged himself; he also broke records for most pull-ups and strongman competitions.

This would soon be challenged as he went in for a regular medical visit in 2010. The doctor noticed a problem during the checkup, and soon Goggins was diagnosed as having an atrial septal defect. This meant he had a hole in his heart. This meant his heart worked at about 75% of capacity. Since he had the condition from when he was born, it meant that his health was deteriorating much faster because of how he had lived his life up to that point. With the intense strain he placed on his body, starting with his training to lose weight to join the SEAL, he had been doing things that were often not recommended for people with his condition.

By the time he neared 40, his body was deteriorating – essentially, he was dying. Instead of viewing the diagnosis and problems as a reason to give up, he decided to establish his own rehabilitation routine. He focused on stretching and healing: "I have spent a minimum of two hours a day and as much as 12 hours a day...stretching, etc., every single day." And this approach worked. His bones began to realign themselves and heal from the strain he had placed on them. He was out of the running world for about five years, but he finally recovered enough to get back into what he loved.

His story caught the attention of Jesse Itzler, who owned the Atlanta Hawks. Wanting to learn from the man who had overcome so much, he hired Goggins to teach him the mental fortitude required to overcome so much. From there, Goggins gained a reputation that saw him take his path in an entirely new direction.

There have been ups and downs since this period, but nothing has been quite the challenge he experienced. Yet, he can approach his life with the kind of resilience that seems impossible. His goal these days is much more straightforward, "I feel guilty if I haven't achieved every day."

CONCLUSION

Goggins has developed a name and brand based on a mentality that pushes people to work out of their comfort zone to become the person they want to be. His focus is on his body and physical accomplishment, but it can be applied to many different areas. It took him a couple of decades, but he found what motivated him the most and focused on reaching specific goals. He was not successful at first, and that led to years of feeling defeated. Goggins has overcome some very difficult times by applying this mentality to other areas. He tries to teach others to accomplish this so they can meet their goals, feel happy with their lives, and not just stay in their comfort zones.